Living Peace

CONNECTING YOUR SPIRITUALITY WITH YOUR WORK FOR JUSTICE

By

VICTOR NARRO

CONNECTING
YOUR SPIRITUALITY WITH YOUR
WORK FOR JUSTICE

Other Books by
Victor Narro

Working for Justice: The L.A. Model of Organizing and Advocacy, Edited by Ruth Milkman, Joshua Bloom and Victor Narro. Cornell University Press (2010)

Undocumented and Unafraid, Edited by Kent Wong, Janna Shadduck-Hernandez, Fabiola Inzunza, Julie Monroe, Victor Narro and Abel Valenzuela Jr. UCLA Center for Labor Research and Education (2012)

Living Peace

CONNECTING
YOUR SPIRITUALITY
WITH YOUR
WORK FOR JUSTICE

By

VICTOR NARRO

Los Angeles, California

Front Cover: Heart mosaic created by the worker cooperative
of the Koreatown Immigrant Workers Alliance of Los Angeles.

Photos by Victor Narro and Laureen Lazarovici Narro

Title ID: 4830469

ISBN: 1499798024
ISBN-13: 978-1499798029

Library of Congress Control Number: 2014910439
CreateSpace Independent Publishing Platform
North Charleston, South Carolina

This book is dedicated to Laureen Lazarovici Narro, my loving partner and co-sojourner in our spiritual journey together

Your love, support and sustenance go way beyond the words I am ever able to put on paper.

Table of Contents

Remember that the people you meet along the way in your journey are dealing with their own hopes and fears. Everyone you meet loves something, has lost something or fears something.

Preface

There are many reasons why this book has become a reality. One major reason is my love for humanity in general, and especially my love for all my brothers and sisters who have dedicated their lives to social justice activism to make this world a better place for everyone. Whether you are a labor activist, an immigrant rights activist, housing or education activist, or an environmental activist, this book is my gift of gratefulness for your commitment and your work in the world.

This book is a challenge for all of us to express and share our spirituality with one another with the hope of making the struggle for justice more compassionate, more fulfilling, more caring, and healthier for all of us. To be an activist for justice is to love humanity, which is a form of spirituality in and of itself. It is time for us to free up the spirituality inside of us, let it come out, and allow it to become a way for our hearts to connect. This book is a guide to help you in that process. This book is designed to help you to read, reflect, and with the help of guidance questions, write about your spirituality. In that sense, it is your spiritual workbook. Through this process, every book will be different. No two books will be alike. Through this book, you can begin shaping a spiritual focus for your activist life that will be unique to you but can be shared with others if you choose to do so. With this book, I am proposing a spiritual awakening where our different forms of spirituality can connect and create a stronger and healthier movement for justice.

Writing this book was a long and challenging spiritual journey for me. With the pages that follow, I am ready to connect my spiritual journey with yours. Before we embark on this journey together, I share with you two words of advice: 1) Read slowly -- very slowly. The passages and reflective questions throughout this book are my attempts to connect with your heart and with your spirituality. Allow any word, phrase or question to trigger a response that causes you to stop, reflect and even re-read. 2) There is no order to this book. You can feel free to skip around from topic to topic, whatever moves you or feels right. Please use the questions to guide you as you reflect on the passage and respond to the questions from your own spiritual foundation. As you reflect on the questions and begin to answer them, you are creating a spiritual journal to record and document your experience of our journey together.

I want to express some special words of acknowledgment. There are many friends, colleagues, teachers, mentors and friends in my work for justice to whom I extend my deepest appreciation for guiding me, supporting me, teaching me, and helping me live out my spirituality in my daily work. The list of names is never ending, and you know who you are. I am the product of the culmination of all your love, wisdom and leadership over the years. Thank you!

Finally, what you write down throughout this book may be so powerful and rewarding that you may want to convert this book into your spiritual notebook that you can refer to over and over again in your daily work as an activist. So read, reflect and find the joy of your spirituality along the way. Now let's begin this special journey together!

Introduction to
My Spirituality

I would like to share with you the elements of my spirituality. The spiritual inspiration of my life as an activist is St. Francis of Assisi. My spirituality does not evolve around St. Francis, the Catholic Saint, but instead it focuses on Francis, the peace activist of the Middle Ages, which is why I refer to him as Francis throughout the book.

Eight hundred years ago, this humble man transformed his world and renewed the Catholic Church by simple but revolutionary acts of practicing his faith as it had never been practiced before. Francis was a man of peace who was known for building bridges of communication, understanding, and cooperation between warring people, groups, and nations.

Francis was born about 1181 into an affluent family during a period of incredible violence and warfare. In his lifetime, the once dominant feudal system was breaking apart, and Italy's provinces and cities were engaged in ongoing strife that led to continuing military conflicts. During his youth, Francis developed a reputation for self-indulgence and playfulness that made him a hero and leader of his town's young people. He watched as his own town of Assisi was wracked by a civil war and a long-running conflict with the nearby town of Perugia. When Francis was 20, the conflict with Perugia erupted into an all-out war. Inspired by patriotism and deep pride, Francis enlisted and went off to battle. He was captured and put in prison for nearly a year.

Two years later, Francis set out for war again, this time as a young knight of a papal army bound for the Crusades. On his way to battle, Francis had a vision that caused him to become weak and very ill. He returned to Assisi, unwilling to take up where he left off. He was ill for almost a year and he struggled with dreams and voices telling him to repair the Church that had fallen. These dreams and visions led him to turn his back on his father's wealthy business and the military heroics of his youth.

Instead, Francis chose a radical life of caring for the poor through his acts of love and humility where he lived among lepers, homeless and others that were neglected by society. Francis was a tough and demanding revolutionary voyager of the human spirit. He was someone who chose to live not with the easy metaphors of poverty, but in real, harsh, grinding "poorness." Francis had a relentless emphasis on real poverty and its necessary companion, humility. Francis was someone who lived his vision. His life (rather than his words) teaches us what it is like to live with spiritual joy in the service of other. Francis was an extraordinary person whose response to the world of the 13th century gives shape and motivation to our response to the world of the 21st.

The spiritual journey with Francis is marked not only by poverty and humility, but by the compassion that is today being rightfully restored to its place at the heart of any viable spirituality. He knew and freely chose a poverty that is politically demanding as well as institutionally challenging. Francis lived a spirituality of compassion rooted in poverty and humility. The way of Francis from the very beginning was the way of peace, love and service.

People of his day believed in him. They wanted to believe in the dream of spiritual freedom that he preached about, and he was proof that it was so. He lived and died quietly and peacefully in Assisi. When the light of the spirit was dying all over the world during the Middle Ages, this little humble person rekindled the flame. This book is my own dream and my own journey with Francis, the human being, lover of all, and peace activist.

One final note: My Franciscan spirituality is a product of my interaction with different spiritual faiths. For example, through my wife Laureen, I was introduced to the spirituality of Thich Nhat Hanh, Vietnamese Buddhist Zen Master, poet, scholar, and human rights activist. My beautiful marriage with Laureen has been the joining together of the spirituality of Francis and Thich Nhat Hanh. Throughout this book, I integrate the insights of Thich Nhat Hanh and the Mindfulness Trainings of his community, Plum Village. I am also a great follower of the spirituality of nonviolence of Mohandas Gandhi and of Native American spirituality. My spirituality is an outcome of all of the above coupled with my strong connection with Francis and his life of activism.

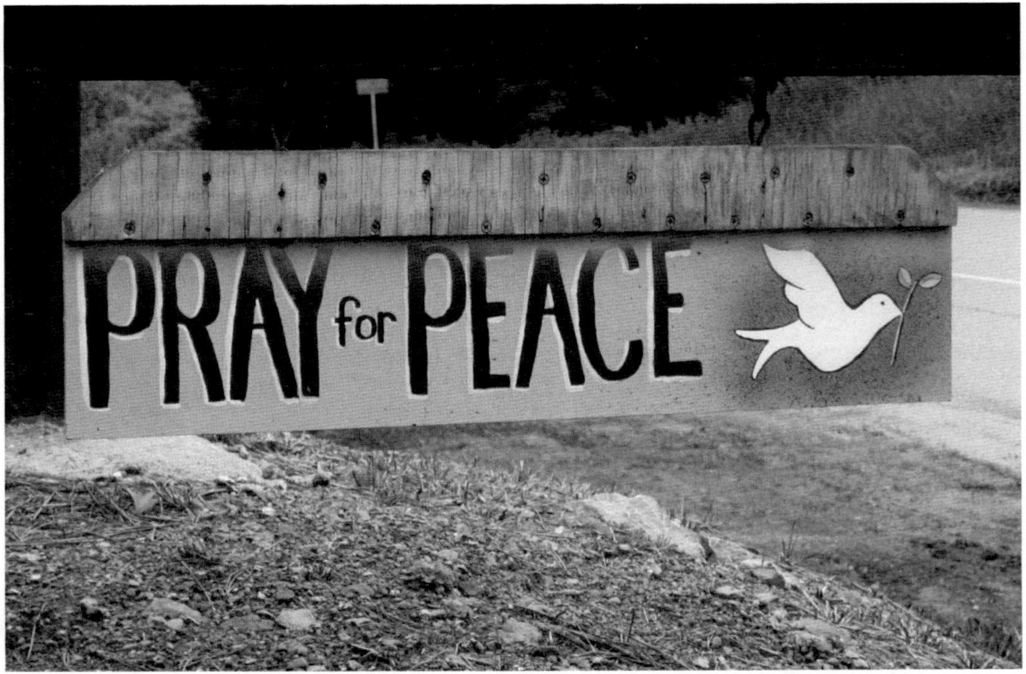
PRAY for PEACE

Francis the Peace Activist

Francis helps me to connect my activism for a better world with my spiritual transformation as a human being. Francis was a person with many weaknesses. He was filled with constant self-doubt about his ability to do what was asked of him by so many. How often in our work for justice do we cast doubt on our abilities and struggle with the fear of moving on to the uncertainty? Francis teaches me that our work as activists is about living fully, which means taking risks, taking losses, sharing the joy of our victories and caring for one other as part of the struggle.

What Francis sought in life was joyful simplicity and not to create a foundation for what would become a worldwide movement to reform the Catholic Church, an institution that was corrupt in his days. He struggled with the growth of the movement that he started and his inability to sustain it and give it direction. It is a struggle that in inherent in all of us as activist leaders and one that we must recognize and embrace.

Francis' teachings can easily be converted to the principles that we try to uphold in our work as activists for justice. My many years of reading about Francis and meditating with him have helped me to learn the Franciscan way of living and integrate it with my life of activism. I walk and converse with Francis everyday as he guides me and teaches me in my daily work as an activist for justice and a human being. Francis is my colleague, friend, and mentor in my daily struggle for social justice.

Reflection Questions

1. **What is your spirituality that connects with your life and your work as an activist?**

2. **How did your spirituality come to evolve to where it is today?**

3. **If you have yet to define your spirituality, what steps can you take to find it?**

Notes

Notes

Notes

Our four walls become for us what they contain.
Go beyond your boundaries and your journey will
become whole.

Meaning of Leadership

Preach always. And if necessary use words.

It makes no sense to walk somewhere to preach if your walking is not your preaching.

— St. Francis

My message is my life.

— Mohandas Gandhi

The message Francis taught was the message he lived. There was no disconnection between his words and his deeds, his public pronouncements and his private life. Witnessing his faith in action helped people to believe. Francis made believers out of many through his acts. For Francis, the measure of a good sermon wasn't based on the rhetoric. As he put it, "There is no better sermon than the practice of the virtues."

A friend and colleague in the movement once mentioned to me that Francis was the first person in history to "walk the talk." While I am not a historian to ascertain the accuracy of this statement, I do consider Francis as a great example of this principle that we so often promote in the work for social justice. These two statements bring to me a reflection of leadership, what it is and what it is not. The term "leadership" is used in so many different ways in the social justice movement. It is a concept that is used so many times, that we have become inured to it. We are often lulled by good, effective rhetoric in the media, at major rallies, at major conferences, etc. The question still lingers for me: What makes a good leader? Francis always talked about how it would make no sense to walk a great distance from town to town to preach the good word unless you preach during each step along the way through your acts. To every town, to everyone, he preached peace. He did not do so with great eloquence and the strength of human reasoning, but with the power of the Spirit. He breached boldly, flattering no one nor making promises. He did not rely on his words, but on the example of his life. He practiced *before* he preached.

A quality of true leadership that connects me with Francis is to let your walking be your rhetoric. My challenge is how to translate this concept into action. It requires a process of fighting off my temptations to please myself before others, to please my sense of ego and self-centeredness, and to please my sense of leaving behind a legacy. These temptations, which I think are dominant throughout the movement, sometimes result in me losing my sense of privileged status as an activist in my community. Shouldn't true leadership be about leading with your acts instead of your rhetoric or leading with your walking instead of your talking? Francis taught me that a good leader understands that leading by acts of unselfishness and humility can help create stronger communities than words alone. Francis was a great orator when he did preach, and words are effective to inspire and move people to action. But acts are where words connect to plight of others. Acts give meaning to words and they create the activism to bring about change to people's lives.

My goal every day is to learn from the life of Francis and apply his lessons to my daily work of social justice activism. My life as a social justice activist is interwoven with my spiritual journey with Francis. Francis in essence is the equivalent of a spiritual campaign director, guiding me as I move forward with fighting for the dignity and well being of others to make justice a reality for them.

1. **What is your perception of leadership?**

2. **What does it mean to you when others see you as a leader?**

Notes

Notes

Notes

The path to your dream loses direction if you forget those who helped and supported you along the way.

Reflection 2:

Our Heart-to-Heart Connection

Blessed is the person who supports his neighbor in his weakness as he would want to be supported were he in a similar situation.

-St. Francis

While you are proclaiming peace with your lips, be careful to have it even more fully in your heart.

-St. Francis

Interconnectedness between all of us in social justice work is an important and indispensable part of an activist life. Francis would spend long hours with each of his brothers that formed the first band of followers of his teachings. He lived the heart-to-heart connections with his group of brothers. Similarly, in the movement for social change, we are all interwoven – ourselves and our lives. Francis had the capacity to go deep into someone's heart and share the joy and sadness of that person. As activists, we have the potential to allow each other's grief and happiness to flow through ourselves. In reaching such a potential of human relationship, we will stir the Goodness inside each of us to become the spiritual focal point from which we are connected. Francis saw love as the driving force that enables us to connect with our Goodness and share it with others. This is true solidarity in action within the social justice movement – sharing our Goodness with each other. It is sharing our struggles, burdens, joy and victories with one another. What keeps our Goodness lively and connected with one another is the spiritual force of love for each other, much in the same way of the unconditional love that Francis had for all of creation.

Thich Nhat Hanh in the Fourth Mindfulness Training, Loving Speech and Deep Listening, shares the following:

Aware of the suffering caused by unmindful speech and the inability to listen to others, I am committed to cultivating loving speech and compassionate listening in order to relieve suffering and to promote reconciliation and peace in myself and among other people, ethnic and religious groups, and nations. Knowing that words can create happiness or suffering, I am committed to speaking truthfully using words that inspire confidence, joy and hope. When anger is manifesting in me, I am determined not to speak. I will practice mindful breathing and walking in order to recognize and to look deeply into its roots, especially in my wrong perceptions and lack of understanding of the suffering in myself and in the other person. I will speak and listen in a way that can help me and the other person to release the suffering and see the way out of difficult situations. I am determined not to spread news that I do not know to be certain and not to utter words that can cause division or discord. I will make daily efforts, in my speaking and listening, to nourish my capacity for understanding, love, joy, and inclusiveness, and gradually transform anger, violence, and fear that lie deep in my consciousness.

We must learn to engage in active listening with our heart, which will then enable us to speak through compassion or loving speech, and not anger, frustration or fear. Really listening, and hearing without judgment, is a gift that we can give to each other to enhance all of our lives. When we are really heard, and the other understands our meaning and emotions, we feel valued and respected: a condition necessary for true love and true happiness. There is a no more precious gift, to give or receive, than to listen to the words of another. This process of active listening and loving speech will enable us to be mindful of and respect the dignity within each one of us.

Along with human dignity, we must also fight for what I call "spiritual dignity." Spiritual dignity is the force that strengthens the element of love within the movement for justice. To be able to fight for the spiritual dignity of others, an activist must be grounded in spirituality – whether it is from religious faith, spiritual beliefs, or a form of compassionate living. We must be mindful at the same time of achieving spiritual dignity of those we are trying to serve and help through our efforts.

As Francis did with his group of followers, we as activists should create our own sense of community that becomes our spiritual incubator that helps us to grow and frees us up to serve. For Francis, the way to live a fulfilling life is to spend it in the service of others, and not trying to hide somewhere where we feel safe and protected. Thomas of Celano, the first biographer of Francis wrote about how Francis was ready to spend himself to be compassionate towards others. For Francis, we are the hands of the creator. We have the freedom to choose healing and love as a way of life. For Francis, spiritual growth leads directly to service. It is incomplete if it focuses only on what it does for you alone. Spirituality that does not reach out beyond ourselves is like a body without hands. Love that is not communicated through demonstrable acts is love unexpressed.

There can be a feeling of emptiness that creeps in when the work of activism becomes a routine of daily activities and tasks. A framework of spirituality enables one to reflect and focus on the interconnectedness that we have with our inner spiritual self and with others around us. Much of our daily work in the movement is about the fragility of life, and not knowing what's going on or what will happen next -- but in the end relying on our inner strength to believe that Life is inherent in everyone we help. This helps us to realize that it is the relationships within our daily work that should become the central focus. There is really no meaning in a task or activity unless there is a deep inter-connection with our spirituality and with one another in our work for social justice.

Reflection Questions

1. How do you connect with your co-workers, colleagues or community members in your daily work for justice?

2. What does it mean to be in solidarity with and connected to one another?

Notes

Notes

Notes

To be truly alive is to be a humble sojourner into the hearts of others and a faithful pioneer of the human soul.

Reflection 3:

Simplicity & Activism

Live simply so that others may simply live.

—Mohandas Gandhi

Francis and his followers have taught me that simplicity is not a specialized discipline. For Francis and his followers, simplicity was the garden from which all spiritual virtues grow, and a prerequisite to us being fully human and spiritual. Simplicity in our lives as activists lies in where we place our hearts and how we shift from our ego center to our spiritual center, where we can connect with our Goodness. Once we are able to make this shift, we find a simple living that enables us to help others from a place of genuine compassion and love, and not from one of self-centeredness disguised as compassion.

Simplicity becomes the soil in my spiritual garden from which my values can grow and develop. The virtue of simplicity allows my acts to be genuine and pure, and coming from the Goodness in my heart and not my ego center. To simplify my life as an activist lies not so much in what I rid myself of as in what I do to focus on my spirit and compassion for giving and sharing.

For Francis the activist, simplicity was fighting for equality in a world of savage disparity. The world of Francis, much like ours today, was one of the mercantile trade economy dominating and taking over the traditional church-run economy of the Middle Ages. Like the global economy of today, this transition to a new economic model during Francis' time created deep social inequalities and disparity of wealth. Much like today's struggle for economic justice, Francis and his followers focused on improving the lives of the poor and homeless victimized by the injustices of this mercantile economy.

This approach of a simple life rooted in Francis' teachings leads me to decrease my emphasis on individualism and self-gratification, and instead increase my awareness of the lives of others and caring for their well-being. For Francis, life simply was the process of being simply for others. What this means is that as activists, we should act for the well-being of others, and not for our self-gratification. This does not mean that we must not praise ourselves for the work that we do as activists. Quite the contrary. We should praise ourselves and one another for the work that we do as activists to improve the lives of others and bring about a just and humane society. This is a great form of self-care.

Reflection Questions

1. **Reflect on an experience where you did something that was transformational for someone or a group. How did it make you feel?**

2. **How are you able to ensure that your acts of helping others are motivated by genuine compassion and love?**

3. **What do you do to praise yourself and those around you in a way that promotes self-care?**

Notes

Notes

The only addiction in your life should be the consumption of giving.

Reflection 4:

Joy and Activism

All the darkness in the world cannot extinguish the flame of a single candle.

-St. Francis

Spiritual joy is a state that Francis always sought to achieve for himself and his brothers. For Francis, spiritual joy is joyful simplicity mixed in with humility and compassion for others. Francis' spiritual joy was fulfilled when he connected with the joy of those around him. He acquired spiritual joy through acts of simplicity with love and compassion towards others in times of need and suffering.

Spiritual joy relies on our interconnectedness. There is greater spirit, a creator, which holds all things together. Thich Nhat Hanh calls this universal belonging "Interbeing." Catholics call it the Holy Spirit. Every atom of our physical bodies was part of some other living or nonliving entity, and will be so again before long. Through our bodies we belong inextricably to all other living beings. All atoms in our flesh and bones have once been in a supernova. What remains unchanged is "the inner body" or "the soul."

This spiritual interconnectedness was essential for Francis to experience true joy. We are all connected to one another. My joy and suffering are connected to your joy and suffering as well as those of others. Like Francis, this spiritual interconnectedness is essential for me to achieve my highest fulfillment in my work as an activist.

When I am part of a campaign by a group of workers to organize a union or to improve working conditions against an abusive employer, my work to help these workers and the joy that they experience in their victories is connected to my spiritual joy. It must be a shared spiritual joy -- the connectedness of our loving and caring for one another. From a standpoint of organizing, this may be seen as the highest level of solidarity. In a way, this presence of sharing one another's joy and suffering becomes a form of solidarity of our spiritual selves.

It is the strength of this collective spiritual joy that creates sustainability for our work as activists as we struggle against the forces of injustice. One of my favorite quotes from Francis is, "All the darkness in the world cannot extinguish the flame of a single candle." That single candle is the coming together of the compassion and love that we come to share with one another during our struggle for justice. That single flame is our collective spiritual joy in action.

Reflection Questions

1. **What meaning does the word "solidarity" have for you?**

2. **Can you reflect on a moment or act of solidarity during your work as an activist? What did you feel?**

Notes

Notes

Better to be poor with humility than rich with selfishness.

Reflection 5:

Humility and Activism

We can never know how patient or humble we are when everything is going well with us. But when those who should cooperate with us do exactly the opposite, then we can know. A person has as much patience and humility as he or she has then, and no more.

- St. Francis

Those who are put in charge of others should be no prouder of their office than if they had been appointed to wash the feet of their [brothers] .

-St. Francis

To be humbled, it is said, strengthens a generous spirit. Like the principles of non-violence, humility in social justice work is not submission or a state of passiveness; rather, it is a powerful force for change. Francis understood that the biggest threat to humility was the power of human pride and ego. For him, humility in its highest form (holy or spiritual humility) always puts pride and ego to shame. By pride, Francis did not talk about the pride in you that is a meaningful way of loving yourself. We must feel proud of our commitment to an activist life and our work to better the lives of others. We must embrace this pride in ourselves as activists for social change, and we must express how much we are proud of our friends and colleagues in the work for social change. This is an important part of self-care and community care within our lives as activists. What Francis teaches us is to protect ourselves against the pride that inflates our egos and selfish desires.

Francis saw humility as the only way to prevent our ego from poisoning our pride. In this way, humility is a form of "self-activism" where we, as activists, take proactive steps to ensure that we act for the act itself, and not to feed our selfish desires or be puffed up by the praises of others. Just as Francis preached a way of life through the principle of humility, we too must approach our work for social justice in the same way. What does this mean? It means that we must exercise humility through acts of compassion and selflessness as we carry out our tasks in our everyday work – in a campaign, in a picket line, a protest, giving a presentation or workshop, representing a client, visiting policy makers, etc. In whatever activity we engage in as part of our activist work, we must always do it through the principle of humility that Francis teaches us.

Humility and the integration of this principle in my daily work as an activist is a daily discipline. It requires a period of reflection and meditation on a daily basis. It requires a cycle of acts of humility followed by reflection and reflection followed by acts of humility. After a period of integrating acts and reflection of humility into my work continually, it becomes a way of life for me as an activist.

Francis lived and preached a radical message of poverty over wealth, powerlessness over power, and serving over ruling with a strong and active influence that provided guidance and leadership for his followers. Francis called his ragtag group of followers the "Order of Friars Minor." His insistence on being "minor" in his way of life was truly revolutionary when you learn about Europe during his day. Europe in the 13th century was in state of transformation from a feudal system, which was dominated by the wealthy and the Church, to a mercantile market economy. It went from a rural agrarian society based on barter to an increasingly urban culture based on cash. People sought higher social standing and to become part of the noble class. Everyone was trying to leap from the class of "minores" (common people status) to "majors" (nobility). It was the historical traces of early capitalism, not unlike today's society that upholds individualism and "getting ahead" over a sense of community. Francis rigorously followed the way of humility in his struggles to create a new society.

My experiences with immigrant families and immigrant workers offer me opportunities to follow the way of humility in my work. Francis teaches me that humility is the process by which we are interconnected with one another. It is our connection to our hearts that enable us to share in the universal Goodness. Through the principle of humility, I am able to connect with each person in my activist work as someone unique with a special set of talents and gifts. Francis teaches me that we are each a unique artwork of the great Artist, our Spirit Creator, who made each of us in his own image. Each of us has something unique to contribute, a special gift. Francis' way of humility enables me to find that special gift and uniqueness in each of us and embrace it.

Self-awareness at all times during our work for justice helps keep us in a state of humility. Self- awareness of how we treat others and how we engage with our colleagues in campaigns and other activities guides us in the community we are trying to build. We must always be in the presence of this self-awareness. Francis teaches me to do so by reciting two prayers. One is the Prayer for Peace, which is the most attributed to St. Francis, but it was not written by him. Its origins in fact go back to the early 20th century. Many scholars believe that it was written anonymously during the end of World War I. I'd like to think it was written by a soldier who fought in the world and survived as a way to reflect and provide a meaningful message for others. The following excerpt from this prayer reflects the Franciscan way of living a life of compassion and service to others, and it helps me maintain the mindfulness of my humility as an activist:

Grant that I may not try to be comforted, but to comfort;

Not try to be understood, but to understand;

Not try to be loved, but to love.

Similarly, the other passage that I use to engage in my daily meditation and reflection is from Brother Giles (c. 1190 – 1262), one of the original companions of Francis. Francis called him "The Knight of our Round Table." In their journeys together, Brother Giles was always at pains to procure by manual labor what food and shelter he needed. A keen observer of those around him, Giles acquired in the course of these travels much valuable knowledge and experience, which he turned to good deeds for others in need. His sermons were brief and heartfelt talks, filled with wisdom. He never minced his words, but spoke to all with the freedom of his heart.

Francis always held this saying from Brother Giles close to his heart:

Blessed are you who love, and don't expect to be loved in return.

Blessed are you who fear, and don't want to be feared.

Blessed are you who serve and don't expect to be served in return.

Blessed are you who treat others well and don't expect like treatment in return.

Applying the teaching of Brother Giles into my practice, I am always mindful of my acts without any expectation for praise or something similar in return.

I act for others out of my love and compassion for them, not because I expect something in return. This is not to say that we don't merit recognition for our work as activists. Praising one another is very much needed in social justice work. Praises of our work are healthy for our self-esteem. Praising one another is important to demonstrate our caring and love for one another. This is a great way to promote community care in the social justice movement. Loving and advocating for yourself is critical in your path towards becoming a true activist. The extent of how much you love and serve others depends on how much you are able to love yourself. It is a healthy form of self love for you to receive recognition and praise for your work.

What we must be careful to avoid, however, is to commit acts and expect praise or recognition to puff up our egos. We must be careful because our egos can be disguised as goodness or compassion. Our ego and selflessness can become so intertwined that we mistake them for one in the same. Humility prevents our healthy self-esteem from slipping into egotism and self-centeredness.

Francis always instructed his group of friars never to "despise or judge people they see dressed in soft and shadowy garments and using choice food or drink, but rather let each one judge and despise himself."

We can't really judge others. What do we know of what others are like on the inside? Someone seems to be bad. What do we know about that person's past experiences, parents, family upbringing, education, emotions, influences, episodes she may have suffered, painful experiences, mental or physical sickness, or other events in her life? We must never judge each other. If you take away the education, life experiences, titles, achievements that we all have, we will realize that each one of us is a human being worthy of love and compassion. We are all the same. We must never judge others. Instead, we must praise them for who they are, their gifts and talents, and wish them our Goodness.

There is a spiritual stream of humility, compassion and love that flows from the Spirit Creator throughout the universe. Let this stream flow through you and help it to flow through others. Be bold and take risks to flow with that stream.

Reflection Questions

1. What steps do you take to praise others who work with you?

2. How are you about receiving praise? What do you feel when others praise you or your work?

3. What does the principle of humility mean for you? How are you able to integrate humility into your activist life and work?

Notes

Notes

To listen to one's own heart when others are saying something different is the hardest test of one's spirit.

Reflection 6:

Compassion and Activism

Remember that when you leave this earth, you can take with you nothing that you have received-- only what you have given.

-St. Francis

Love is a mind that brings peace, joy, and happiness to another person. Compassion is a mind that removes the suffering that is present in the other.

-Thich Nhat Hanh

With all the examples of the life of Francis, along with his wise words, I have come to learn that compassion is not easy or painless, but it is life's most demanding work. We cannot disconnect compassion from our social justice activism. To do so would leave our activist work with an empty void, where we would fill it up with our self-centeredness and our egos.

Francis teaches me that through compassion we are able to live and experience each other's joy, happiness, grief and difficulties. Compassion begins with a communication that is genuine and heart to heart (not mind to mind). It involves speaking from the heart and actively listening from the heart. When you have this type of conversation with someone, the two hearts are joined and a true moment of compassion has taken place. Remember that the people you meet along the way in your work for justice are dealing with their own hopes and fears. Everyone you meet loves something, has lost something or is in fear of something.

Francis teaches me a different approach to dealing with our conflicts and disagreements, an approach based on his spiritual life of compassion, charity, gentleness, and love. Francis did not see the world in terms of good vs. bad, sinners vs. saints. Instead, he saw the world as every human being deserving love and respect. Francis' approach to compassion is living a life of non-violence and instilling this virtue in others. This approach is active and not passive. An activist life of non-violence and acts of compassion is a powerful force for justice. Can you imagine if each one of us as activists were to live by and carry out our work for justice with this approach? We would create such a powerful force that could overcome any evil or injustice that may come our way. The best example of how Francis embraced a life of compassion was his experience with lepers.

During the Middle Ages, there was no cure for leprosy. The practice in those days was to isolate lepers into their own colonies. The thought was that this isolation would help prevent the spread of the disease. For most of history, people with leprosy suffered alone in these isolated colonies, shut off by society. Francis grew up with a strong distaste for lepers. He grew up in what would be the equivalent of the 1 percent today. He father was a wealthy merchant who made a fortune in the emerging mercantile economy that would eventually replace the one based on the feudalism of the Middle Ages. It is said that the young Francis would look at the houses of lepers from two miles away and would pinch his nostrils with his fingers in disgust.

While riding his horse one day, Francis came across a leper on the road. He felt uncomfortable and nauseous as he got closer to the leper. Instead of riding away and evading the encounter however, a strange feeling inside made Francis stay on the path towards the leper. He got off his horse, walked up to the leper and kissed him on the cheek. Soon thereafter, Francis would move to the leper colony and would begin caring for them and washing their wounds. Something powerful happened at that moment when Francis got off his horse and kissed the leper. He broke through his barrier of comfort and reached out to a person in an unfamiliar situation with love and compassion. He listened to his heart and connected with the leper's heart instead of giving in to his fears and doubts. This act of compassion was the beginning of a journey for Francis that started a movement for peace, good and justice. Whenever Francis would see a poor person, he would reach out with unconditional love and compassion to help.

Francis' compassion for those around him was more than an issue of mind and thought. It was a matter of his heart. He transferred to his heart the afflictions of those who were poor and sick. Francis believed that compassion, if it has any meaning at all, needed to be translated into action. You must first have peace in your heart before you can become an advocate for peace in the world.

Reflection Questions

1. What do you do to promote compassion and non-violence in your work for justice?

2. Have you ever had an experience of witnessing acts compassion and non-violence in your work?

3. Have you ever encountered a moment of true compassion in your work? What happened? How did it make you feel?

Notes

Notes

True leadership is about having the humility to step back and allow others to step forward.

Reflection 7:

Spiritual Poverty in Our Journey of Activism

"Let us look at wealth and poverty. The affluent society and the deprived society inter-are. The wealth of one society is made of the poverty of the other. Wealth is made of non-wealth elements, and poverty is made by non-poverty elements. So we must be careful not to imprison ourselves in concepts. The truth is that everything contains everything else. We cannot just be, we can only inter-be. We are responsible for everything that happens around us."

-Thich Nhat Hanh

Remember that when you leave this earth, you can take with you nothing that you have received-- only what you have given.

-St. Francis

Much has been written about Francis' life of poverty. He often spoke of how, when he got married, he would choose the most beautiful and worthy bride to be his wife. At the time, no one knew that he was referring to his love of Lady Poverty. It was said that Francis chose a life of extreme poverty to the detriment of his body's health, which was why he died of severe illnesses at the age of 45. There is much interpretation of what Francis tried to teach us about spiritual poverty. In fact, he wrote little about it and when he did, he was pointing to the humility of how we approach the inequality of wealth and issues of poverty. For Francis, the "spirit of poverty" was the attitude of being free, not enslaved by money and what money can buy.

Franciscan poverty teaches us to live our lives with the things we really need, instead of letting our desires for luxury control our life. Franciscan poverty flees from luxury and loves the things that give less pleasure to the ego and to vanity. If he were alive today, Francis would tell us that we should be cheerful, glad, and perfectly willing not to have the latest car, the fanciest clothing or the most expensive house. He would tell us that there is nothing wrong with what pleases the eye or our sense of aesthetics. The danger, he would tell us, is in the vanity, the conceit, the greed that often lurks beneath. Francis today would be shocked at how our society is characterized by impulse-buying and consumerism. He would condemn the wasteful buying of luxuries, duplicates, gadgets, and how the greed of banking institutions and corporations has led the highest disparity between the rich and the poor than ever before in history.

Thich Nhat Hanh recites the following in his Second Mindfulness Training, True Happiness:

Aware of the suffering caused by exploitation, social injustice, stealing, and oppression, I am committed to practicing generosity in my thinking, speaking, and acting. I am determined not to steal and not to possess anything that should belong to others; and I will share my time, energy, and material resources with those who are in need. I will practice looking deeply to see that the happiness and suffering of others are not separate from my own happiness and suffering; that true happiness is not possible without understanding and compassion; and that running after wealth, fame, power and sensual pleasures can bring much suffering and despair. I am aware that happiness depends on my mental attitude and not on external conditions, and that I can live happily in the present moment simply by remembering that I already have more than enough conditions to be happy. I am committed to practicing Right Livelihood so that I can help reduce the suffering of living beings on Earth and reverse the process of global warming.

Moreover, Thich Nhat Hanh addresses the issue of poverty in the following excerpt on the spiritual practice of generosity which comes under kindness.

"Practicing generosity means continually acting in a way that will help equalize the difference between the wealthy and the impoverished. Whatever we do to ease human suffering and create social justice can be considered practicing generosity. How can a person practicing 'knowing how to feel satisfied with few possessions' also practice generosity? It is by living simply. Almost everyone who spends his or her life serving and helping others, sacrificing themselves for the sake of humanity, lives simply. If they live their lives worrying about making money and gaining merit, how can they practice generosity? Mahatma Gandhi lived a very simple life; nevertheless his merit helping humanity and saving human beings was immeasurable. There are thousands of people among us who live very simply, while being very helpful to many, many others. They do not have as great a reputation as Gandhi, but their merit is no less than his. It is enough for us just to be a little more attentive and aware of the presence of people like these. They do not practice generosity by giving money that they do not possess, but rather by giving their time, energy, love, and care — their entire lives."

What does all this mean to me as an activist? Francis referred to humility as the sister of spiritual poverty. The principle of humility creates the space within our heart to be filled with spiritual poverty. Spiritual poverty does not mean giving up all belongings and sacrificing ourselves in a way that is unhealthy. Instead, spiritual poverty enables us to be well grounded as activists so that our activist work promotes love and compassion in a way that is not driven by selfish desires. As activists, when we integrate spiritual poverty into our daily tasks and activities, we are able to find the love and compassion that creates meaningful changes in the lives of others. With this approach, we find that behind every task or activity is a human connection. Through a presence of spiritual poverty, we are able to put the human relationship before the task. Achieving spiritual poverty means that every aspect of our work is driven by our love and compassion for others. Our goals and the process of getting there will be one in the same, where every step we take becomes an act of love and compassion.

For Francis, he referred to the journey and the dream as being one in the same. Francis was only 45 years old when he died, but he left behind a spiritual dream and a life journey that is a challenge for all of us. He lived in spiritual poverty every day all the way to his last breath. He lived a peace and joy that surpasses all understanding. For him, the journey and the dream of his spiritual life were of the same source of love and both were truly alive within his heart. Imagine what kind of social justice movement we would have if every step in the process of carrying out our work was driven by an act of love and compassion through our hearts, and not our minds.

Finally, spiritual poverty combined with humility creates space in our hearts for forgiveness. An unforgiving spirit blocks the flow of grace and mercy into our lives, causing us to live in a stagnant state of regrets, animosities and grudges. Forgiveness simply means releasing those who have offended you from your own hostility and anger. It is the freedom of no longer holding anguish or bitterness inside you. It does not change the act that caused you harm or pain. Forgiveness creates room in your heart for love and mercy, which are necessary for bringing peace in the world.

1. **What does spiritual poverty mean for you? Is there something comparable in your spirituality or religious faith?**

2. **Have you had an experience where, in carrying out your work, a human connection or relationship became a priority before a task or activity?**

Notes

Notes

In the work for justice we are always engaged in the process of planning ahead. Nothing really happens tomorrow unless we take the time to appreciate one another today.

Self-Care and Activism

You learn to speak by speaking, to study by study-ing, to run by running, to work by working; and just so, you learn to love by loving. All those who think to learn in any other way deceive themselves.

- St. Francis

Until we are able to love and take care of our-selves, we cannot be of much help to others.

-Thich Nhat Hanh

Francis found a balance between solitude and service, between separation from the world and an intense dedication to living in it for the sake of others. Francis balanced intense contemplation with loving service to the world. Francis understood that the dichotomy between solitude and service is a false one, because everyone needs both. If we don't spend time alone to reflect and meditate, we can become spiritually weak, and our work in the world carries little of lasting value. On the other hand, if we spend all our time in reflection and meditation, we may become spiritually isolated and self-contained. Francis was considered by many as a deeply loving mystic. He presented us with a picture of the life-giving balance between prayer or meditation and service.

In his Fifth Mindfulness Training, Nourishment and Healing, Thich Nhat Hanh states the following:

Aware of the suffering caused by unmindful consumption, I am committed to cultivating good health, both physical and mental, for myself, my family, and my society by practicing mindful eating, drinking, and consuming. I will practice looking deeply into how I consume the Four Kinds of Nutriments, namely edible foods, sense impressions, volition, and consciousness. I am determined not to gamble, or to use alcohol, drugs, or any other products which contain toxins, such as certain websites, electronic games, TV programs, films, magazines, books, and conversations. I will practice coming back to the present moment to be in touch with the refreshing, healing and nourishing elements in me and around me, not letting regrets and sorrow drag me back into the past nor letting anxieties, fear, or craving pull me out of the present moment. I am determined not to try to cover up loneliness, anxiety, or other suffering by losing myself in consumption. I will contemplate interbeing and consume in a way that preserves peace, joy, and well-being in my body and consciousness, and in the collective body and consciousness of my family, my society and the Earth.

What does this mean for me as an activist? As activists, it is upon us to find our unique balance between solitude and service. We must find this balance for ourselves, our families, our friends, and our community. Our spaces for self-reflection and self-retreat become a critical part of our work for justice. Each of us needs a balance of solitude and service. We need to disconnect and enter into our own periods of self-reflection and spiritual renewal in order to have lasting meaningful impact as activists for justice. It is the life-giving balance between retreat and reflection (meditation or prayer), and service. As activists, we must find our own unique balance between solitude and service. We have special gifts as activists that we must share with others. Going into our personal spaces for reflection and meditation keeps us mindful of our special gifts and how we must share them.

My daily meditation and refection with Francis serves as a spiritual incubator that helps me grow and frees me up to serve others. Francis wanted nothing more in his life than to spend himself in order to be compassionate towards others. This mindfulness is similar to Thich Nhat Hanh's concept of "interbeing." To apply it to us as activists, there is the connection between our mind, our heart and our sense of justice, which lies deep within our heart. We become truly alive as activists once we make this connection and it then leads to the interconnectedness between our heart and the hearts of those around us.

Francis was very hard on his body. He punished himself and denied his health as an expression and commitment of his spirituality and his faith. It was not until later near the end of his life when he was dying from diseases, many of which were caused by his neglect of his health and body, he apologized to "Brother Ass," which was how he referred to his body. Before he died, he preached to his followers never to abuse their bodies in the same way. As activists, we are constantly facing the dilemma of extending ourselves emotionally, physically and spiritually because of the great demands placed upon us by communities in need of justice. We are also consumed by the "self martyr" syndrome where the measurement of our commitment to our justice work is determined by how much we sacrifice of our bodies, health and our relationships with loved ones.

What Francis taught us when he was living out his last days was that we must not sacrifice ourselves to the level of jeopardizing our healthy bodies, healthy lives, and healthy balance. Francis died at age 45, but his body was broken and in significant ill-health when he was ten years younger. I always imagine how much more he would have been able to do had he taken care of his body and health, which would have enabled him to live for many more years. Our ability to do our work for social justice is reliant on our physical capacity and our health. There should be no disconnection here. If we are unhealthy, we are limited to what we are able to do as activists. Healthy body, mind and spirit should equate healthy activism.

Reflection Questions

1. **What does it mean for you to achieve a healthy balance between your mind and body, spirit, family, friends, and community?**

2. **What do you do to maintain this balance and ensure sustainability in your work as an activist?**

Notes

Notes

When surrounded by a thousand dangers, let us not lose heart, except to make room for one another in our hearts.

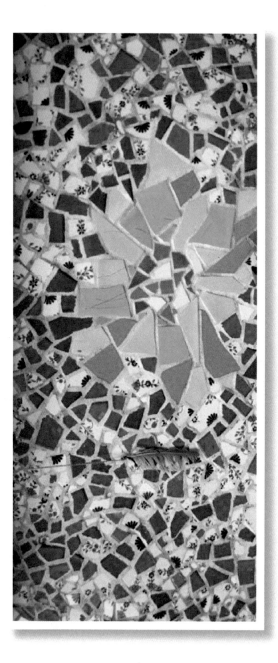

Reflection 9:

Creativity and Activism

He who works with his hands is a laborer.

He who works with his hands and his head is a craftsman.

He who works with his hands and his head and his heart is an artist.

-St. Francis

In order to have a real relationship with our creativity, we must take the time and care to cultivate it. Our creativity will use this time to confront us, to confide in us, to bond with us, and to plan.

-Julia Cameron, The Artist's Way

In addition to praying and preaching, Francis composed poems and songs, staged dramas and did paintings and sculptures. His life inspired painters, composers and other artists to soar to creative heights. The creativity of Francis and his followers helped influence the beginnings of the Renaissance. The best artists and poets from that era—including Michelangelo—were Franciscans.

Francis teaches me that creativity comes with humanity. All of us were created to create. We must see ourselves as creative human beings, and in the work of social justice, as creative activists. As creative activists, we have to open up spaces both within ourselves and with one another to enable our creativity to flourish. Whether it is music, art, theater, poetry or sports, our creativity must be connected with our work for social justice. Nowhere have I seen creativity flourish more in our movement than with youth activists and worker centers. Groups like worker centers have introduced and integrated puppets, drummers, posters, murals and other artwork into the movement. They have brought out the creativity of their members – workers, students and community members. Similarly, young activists have used spoken word, music, art and other forms of creativity to energize the movement. Community-based worker cooperatives have also created forms of art that we often use in the social justice movement.

There is a Spirit Creator, a higher Goodness or Love, that created the universe, which led to the creation of us all. Creativity is the Spirit Creator's gift to us. We are born with the potential for creativity. Nothing is more empowering for the dignity of a person than to enable that person to use his or her creativity to better the lives of others. As Francis embarked on his spiritual journey, he incorporated his creative spark in his new life. Where he once paraded the streets of Assisi singing the song of troubadours and chivalry, later on he did so with a group of singing friars, singing the lyrics of his newfound spiritual life. This unique and creative approach to his spirituality became Francis' way of life. It was one of tremendous bursts of creativity in the midst of travels, preaching, and visits to many cities. Francis was a singer, poet and musician. He was not an artist by profession, but he believed in his potential to use creativity to express his spiritual faith and teachings. Like Francis, we too can use our creativity within us to fight for social justice. We have this gift inside of us that makes each of us unique in a special way. Our commitment to social justice enables us to find this creativity inside of us and use it in our work as activists.

Francis called his first group of friars the "Jongleurs de Dieu." Jongleurs were jesters or jugglers during the Middle Ages who entertained people by bringing a moment of comic relief. Francis went from singing about his tales of knighthood to becoming a jester and troubadour for peace in the lives of others. He used his creativity to serve his new calling in life. We can do the same for our work as activists. We can become jesters and troubadours in the fight for what is good and just in society.

Francis saw the Artist in the art. He saw the Maker in all that was made and created. He rejoiced in the works of the Spirit Creator and he worked through them to see the source of their being and their life. To Francis, all things were good because they were created by Goodness itself.

We are artists in the movement. We seek justice and love in society through the Goodness that lies in our hearts. We must explore and express our creative selves in our work as social justice activists. It is what we were meant to do. Organizers and activists are musicians, poets, artists, theater performers, and more. Being an activist for social justice is Goodness itself and, as such, we must allow the creativity inside each one of us to flourish and we must allow spaces for others to express their creativity. This is an important aspect of social justice work. To be truly creative and allow our creativity to flourish goes hand in hand with our dignity.

The way we strive to ensure the respect and dignity of others must also include the space for individuals to be able to "live out" their creativity. Each of us should be able to live our own creative lives. It is our creativity that connects us to our wholeness, our Goodness, which then connects us to the ultimate Goodness of the universe. This should be a pathway in our fight for social justice.

Think of a way where you can use your creativity to transform the world around you. You can begin with something basic and build upon it. What is important is that the creative person inside you will become part of your activism. We were created to create, and in expressing our creative selves through our work for justice, we are allowing for others to become creative in their lives, as part of their dignity. Look inward, and unleash your inner artist!

Reflection Questions

1. **What are you doing to allow your creativity to flourish in your work for justice? Is it through music, poetry, theater, or other forms of artistic expression?**

2. **What are you doing in your activist work to enable others to express their creativity?**

Notes

Notes

You must first have Peace in your heart before you can become an agent of Peace in the world.

Spiritual Tools for Your Journey

We should seek not so much to pray but to become prayer.

-St. Francis

In mindfulness one is not only restful and happy, but alert and awake. Meditation is not evasion; it is a serene encounter with reality.

Thich Nhat Hanh

During my years of activism work, I have been blessed with opportunities to learn from great teachers on the application of different tools to enhance my spirituality. As activists, it is important to share how we are implementing our spirituality in our work. Whether it is silent meditation, praying, group reflection, or other practices, we must share and learn from one another to enrich spirituality in the social justice movement. The following are spiritual tools that I have learned over the years from great mentors in the movement.

Reflection Circle

The circle is an ancient, primal symbol. To Native Americans, the symbol represents something that is sacred and holy. It represents unity, strength, protection, infinity, and spirituality. Thus, it is used in ritual, religion, art, architecture, ceremony, and social interaction. Native myth and ritual function according to the cycles of nature and life which is reflected in a circle. A circle is a powerful tool for meaningful spiritual reflection, dialogue, and communication to enhance deep solidarity.

Talking Stick

A growing number of people recognize the talking stick as a powerful tool for facilitating meaningful conversation. To fully actualize the power of this medicine tool involves recognizing, communicating and engaging its full potential for encouraging individual growth, meaningful conversation, and group healing. The power of the talking stick stems from its history and the authority we bestow upon it. Its history includes countless cultures and communities over many generations who granted meaning to such items as a stick, staff, feather or other artifact. Today, we use it to engage in meaningful group planning or problem-solving. The talking stick also has a contemporary history in which activists, counselors, educators, human resource managers and others have been using it to facilitate authentic and meaningful conversations.

Walking Meditation

Walking meditation is a form of meditation in action. In walking meditation, we use the experience of walking as our focus. We become mindful of our experience while walking, and try to keep our awareness involved with the experience of walking. There are several different kinds of walking meditation. We have to be aware of things outside of ourselves and there are many other things outside of ourselves that we will be more aware of than when we are doing sitting meditation – especially if we sit inside. These include the wind, the sun, and the rain; and the sounds of nature and of humans and machines. The practice of walking meditation can fit in to the gaps in our lives quite easily. Even walking from the car into the supermarket can be an opportunity for a minute's walking meditation.

Reflection Questions

1. Are you engaged in any type of individual or group practice that enhances your spirituality?

2. Do you have a form of spiritual practice that you can write about and share with others?

Notes

Notes

Notes

Conclusion and Beginning of Our Journey

Start by doing what is necessary, then what is possible, and suddenly you are doing the impossible.

-St. Francis

I hope you have enjoyed this book and our journey through it together. Please continue forward with your spiritual journey so it can grow to become an inherent part of your life as an activist for justice. I see the ending of this book as the beginning of connecting ourselves as activists through our spirituality. I look forward to creating next steps on moving this work forward.

The pages of this book are never ending. Your participation has helped enrich me and it has created more to the book than when you first opened it. I look forward to our journey together to promote spirituality in the work for justice. Thank you for who you are and what you do, and for allowing our hearts to connect with one another!

Remember that your spiritual journey begins within your heart. We are all born with the capacity to love because we all come from a higher Good. We were created by Goodness itself. Your spiritual journey allows you to find the love that is hidden or worn out by the forces of greed, self- centeredness, and other unhealthy qualities. Humility and compassion become your spiritual tools to help you find the love in your heart and share it with others. Spirituality is not meant to be for your own self-absorption. For your spirituality to have meaning, you must let it "grow out." It must be part of your life of living through compassion. Your spirituality must reach out to others.

Finally, I leave you with an excerpt from a teaching from the great Jewish thinker, Rabbi Tarfon, as translated by Rabbi Rami Shapiro. I always share with my UCLA students during my last day of class with them:

You are not obligated to complete the work,
but neither are you free to abandon it.

Do not be daunted
by the enormity of the world's grief.
Do justly, now.
Love mercy, now.
Walk humbly, now.

Sources

Bodo, Murray, O.F.M. *Francis: The Journey and the Dream*. Cincinnati, Ohio: St. Anthony Messenger Press, 2011.

Bodo, Murray, O.F.M. *The Way of St. Francis: The Challenge of Franciscan Spirituality for Everyone*. Cincinnati, Ohio: St Anthony Messenger Press, 1995.

Foley, Leonard, O.F.M., Jovian Weigel, O.F.M., and Patti Normile, S.F.O. *To Live as Francis Lived: A Guide for Secular Franciscans*. Cincinnati, Ohio: St. Anthony Messenger Press, 2000.

Kirvan, John. *Peace of Heart: Francis of Assisi*. Notre Dame, Indiana: Ave Maria Press, 2009

Pitchford, Susan. *Following Francis: The Franciscan Way for Everyone*. New York: Morehouse Publishing, 2006.

Shapiro, Rabbi Rami M. *Wisdom of the Jewish Sage*. New York: Bell Tower, 1993.

Sweeney, Jon M. *Light in the Dark Ages: The Friendship of Francis and Clare of Assisi*. Massachusetts: Paraclete Press, 2007.

Sweeney, Jon M. *The Road to Assisi: The Essential Biography of St. Francis by Paul Sabatier*. Massachusetts: Paraclete Press, 2003.

Talbot, John Michael, and Steve Rabey. *The Lessons of St. Francis: How to Bring Simplicity and Spirituality Into Your Life*. New York: Plume, 1998.

Thich Nhat Hanh. *Plum Village Chanting and Recitation Book*. Berkeley California: Parallax Press, 2000.

Ugolino di Monte Santa Maria. *The Little Flowers of St. Francis of Assisi*. Trans. W. Heywood. New York: Vintage Books, 1998.

About the Author

Victor Narro has been an advocate for immigrant rights and low-wage workers for thirty years. Working with the UCLA Downtown Labor Center, he provides leadership programs for immigrant workers and internship opportunities for students. He also teaches and lectures at UCLA's Labor and Workplace Studies Program, Chicano/a Studies Department, School of Urban Planning, and Law School.

Involved in policy and organizing campaigns, Narro has written many articles on immigrant and low-wage workers' rights. He is coauthor of *Broken Laws, Unprotected Workers: Violations of Employment and Labor Laws in America's Cities* and *Wage Theft and Workplace Violations in Los Angeles*. He is coeditor of *Working for Justice: The L.A. Model of Organizing and Advocacy.*

Narro promotes harmony and healing throughout the social justice movement as the facilitator of

Native American "talking stick" circles. In *Living Peace: Connecting Your Spirituality with Your Work for Justice,* he brings his passion for the spirituality of St. Francis of Assisi to the social justice movement.

Made in the USA
Monee, IL
31 May 2022